ANTERBURY COLL

From Dawn To Dusk
at the
Donkey Sanctuary

FROM DAWN TO DUSK
at the
DONKEY SANCTUARY

◆

Dr Elisabeth D. Svendsen M.B.E.

with photographs by Dan Bryan and Len Shepherd

◆

Whittet Books

First published 1999
© 1999 by The Donkey Sanctuary
Photographs © 1999 by Dan Bryan and Len Shepherd
Printed in Hong Kong by Wing King Tong Co. Ltd.

Whittet Books Limited, Hill Farm, Stonham Road, Cotton, Stowmarket, Suffolk IP14 4RQ

Len Shepherd took the photographs on pages 6, 15, 30, 43, 48 (top left), 55 (both), 56, 58, 59
Dan Bryan took all the other photographs

British Library Cataloguing in Publication Data
A catalogue record for this book is available from the British Library.

ISBN 1 873580 44 4

The Donkey Sanctuary is at Sidmouth Devon EX10 0NU
Tel (01395) 578222
Fax (01395) 579266
Registered Charity No 264818

Foreword

I must have the most wonderful and rewarding job in the world! Every day is filled with challenges, and each one is totally different - some days are filled with happy moments, others with despair; but one thing gives me the most pleasure every time - being with the donkeys!

As you can't share these moments with me, I thought it would be nice if you could see for yourself some of the daily events at the Sanctuary. Almost 8,000 donkeys have passed through our doors. Not one donkey has been turned away, neither has one been put down unless the quality of life has gone, and in that event this has been carried out in quiet, ideal conditions, their last memory being of a tasty ginger nut biscuit!

(LEFT) Dan, who took most of the photographs in the book, struggles to photograph donkeys who really want a cuddle.

It was not always easy for the two photographers - donkeys are very inquisitive, and love to join in!

There are no distressing photographs. This is a happy book, and the only photograph depicting any cruelty is that of Lorcan on page 41. I didn't think you would want any pictorial evidence of some of the cases of neglect and cruelty we have to deal with, which is when I despair at man's inhumanity to animals.

I hope you will relax and share with me a day at the Donkey Sanctuary.

Dr Elisabeth D Svendsen, M B E

(RIGHT) ... and Len, who also took photographs for the book, takes time off to thank one of his models.

It's dawn at the Donkey Sanctuary, and long before the staff arrive the elderly donkeys in the main yard are eagerly awaiting their breakfasts.

(RIGHT) Coming in for a special breakfast.

At 7.45 a.m. the two night watchmen leave, having filled in the night log book and handed over to the day staff.

Their first job is to feed the elderly donkeys, and soon the buckets are being distributed to their eager recipients.

Other groups of donkeys are also getting special feeds. The group of blind donkeys look forward to being shown to their buckets by their companions, and both friends feed together.

(BELOW) Extra feed for donkeys under special care.

In the Isolation Unit (part of which is shown left) the new arrivals watch warily as the staff move gently among them, feeding them and checking for signs of ill health. Many donkeys receive the special treats they had been used to in their previous homes. It is essential during this period of change that the new arrivals' diets are as similar as possible to that provided previously, in order to reduce stress.

At the Sidmouth Centre of The Elisabeth Svendsen Trust for Children and Donkeys, the arena is being dampened down and the play area set up in readiness for the arrival of the children. The donkeys chosen for the day's work are being brought in to be groomed and fed. The grooms have to wear special clothes and breathing equipment because of the dust and to comply with Health and Safety regulations.

In the fields on the eleven outlying farms - around 1,800 acres in total - the fit donkeys begin grazing. They seem to find the grass particularly tasty when the early morning dew is on it, and the specially selected types of grass sown in the fields provide an adequate and tasty diet, further enhanced by ad lib straw with a little hay in the feeders to top up their fibre diet.

By 8 a.m. the first rounds by
the veterinary staff have begun,
any special problems during
the night having been reported.

(LEFT) Michael Crane, our senior vet, inspects a donkey, closely watched by our Mexican farrier, Marco, here for training.

On Slade House Farm a veterinary visit to New Barn is always on the agenda, as this is where the 'geriatrics' are housed. This group, aged between 30 and 50 years are happily living out their retirement, tended with skill and love. Many could tell heartbreaking stories, but now they are content, being kept warm, cosy and well fed during the winter, and peacefully grazing and dozing away their days during the summer.

Every day at the Sanctuary is different, and the donkeys are well aware of any change in routine. When the farrier arrives many wait patiently for their turn, obligingly lifting their hooves for the farrier's attention.

(ABOVE) Some find it all a bit amusing!

Once a month is weighing day and the donkeys keep a watchful eye as the electronic scales are put into place. Each donkey is quietly encouraged to walk on in turn, to stand and be weighed.

When necessary, following evidence of worm infestation by our laboratory, a dose of worm paste is also given - not always appreciated by the recipients!

To keep the donkeys healthy our team of four vets and five nurses are kept very busy, and our laboratory provides valuable information by non-intrusive research. With over 7,500 donkeys taken into care in the UK there is always plenty to do, and preventative medicine is an important part of our strategy. Many newly arrived donkeys, coming from homes where owners have simply grown too old to care for them, have a real overweight problem - reducing this has to be a really slow programme, otherwise the obese donkey will die due to stress as a result of the combination of leaving its owner and a change of diet. A reduction of ten kilos per annum is sufficient.

All stallions coming into the Sanctuary have to be castrated for two reasons, the obvious one being to prevent unwanted foals. The less obvious reason is to improve their behaviour so they can fit in on a 'long term' basis with a group of donkeys. On arrival they go in a special group of donkeys in the Isolation Unit for six weeks, and they have to be exercised daily (LEFT).

Once cleared from the Unit they stay in a special area until the vets are sure they are fit for the operation, which is carried out in our donkey hospital (RIGHT). Wherever possible their donkey companion goes with them to reduce any stress.

(INSET) Our laboratory technician at work.

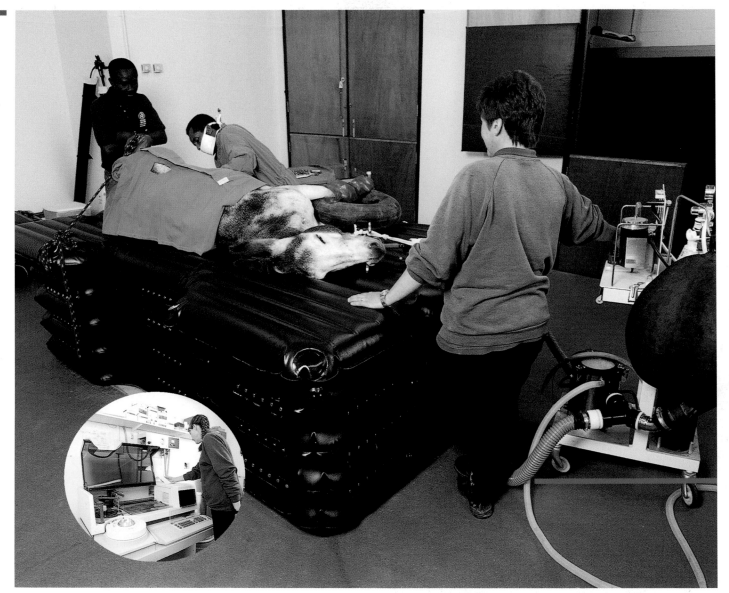

Although we never breed at the Sanctuary, some mares arrive in foal, and the resulting birth gives pleasure not only to us, but to the many visitors who visit daily from all around the world.

(LEFT) Good pals can even share a meal.

(LEFT) Mother and baby doing well.

(RIGHT) I feel frisky.

Donkey Week is the peak of visitor infiltration! Up to 300 donkey lovers arrive and spend a week visiting the farms and cuddling and grooming the donkeys - I don't know who enjoys it the most!

Young, fully fit donkeys are chosen to work with the Elisabeth Svendsen Trust for Children and Donkeys (E.S.T). They really enjoy close contact with children with special needs. Since the first Centre was built, thousands of rides have been given, and close contact made with the donkeys, with not one child being bitten or kicked.

The donkeys have an enormous empathy with these children and visiting our Centres brings new challenges and achievements for the hundreds of youngsters who visit.

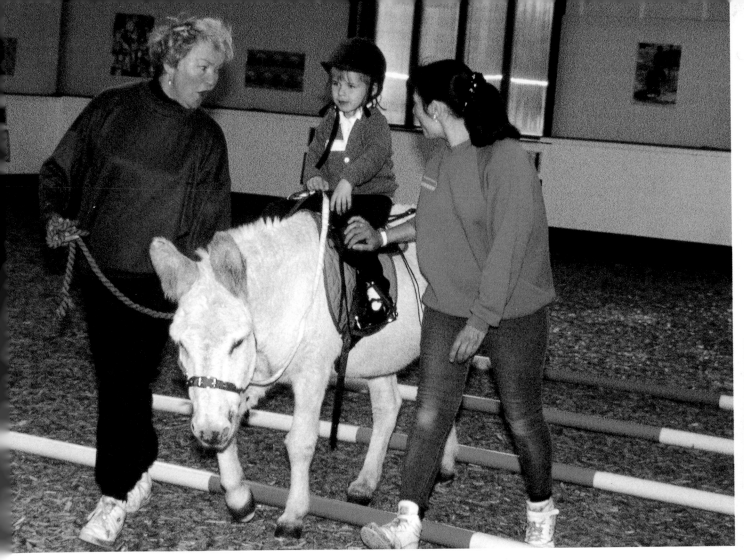

Some children are too heavy to ride the donkeys, so carts are provided for them to learn driving or simply to enjoy the gentle movement.

(LEFT) Training the donkeys can get quite complicated, especially with a 'four in hand'.

Some of the E.S.T donkeys are 'adopted' by members of the public under the adoption scheme. This enables them to enjoy a special asociation with 'their donkey'. The adopted donkeys receive many birthday and Christmas cards, which are attached to the outside wall of the recipient's stable - if they are placed within reach they seem to be accepted as an extra addition to their daily menu!

(RIGHT) Donkeys in the adoption scheme at the E.S.T Centre, Sidmouth: (from left to right) Megan, Dominic, Daniel P. and Tom.

Many volunteers help at the
E.S.T Centres.

For those who cannot get to one of the Centres the E.S.T lorry takes donkeys to visit special schools, which brings smiles to many young faces.

Two great characters arrived during 1998 - Merlin and Susie Tangye (LEFT). These were the famous donkeys featured by Derek Tangye in his books on Cornish country life, which have brought pleasure to many people. After Mr Tangye's death, Merlin and Susie came into our care and have settled in well, enjoying all the fuss and attention they receive from our visitors. Merlin and Susie are inseparable, and one day it was touching to see Merlin, who had decided to go into the big barn to sample the hay, stop half way across the yard when he realised that Susie wasn't behind him. He turned around and, determinedly gripping her collar, he set off for the barn again!

This Stable Donated By
BERYL BRUCE LATHAM

8

Donkeys form close associations and become inseparable friends, grazing together, eating together and, in the event of necessary veterinary care, supporting each other. For blind donkeys (ABOVE) the relationship is of mutual benefit. Friendships are so close that when, unfortunately, one dies, the friend has to be allowed at least one hour alone with its dead companion to take in what has happened. If this is not done, the friend can actually die as well, as it will spend day after day looking for its companion to no avail.

With a big bray and big ears, donkeys can communicate with friends, even from one of our farms to another!

A human friend can be as good as a donkey friend, especially when it makes a fuss of you!

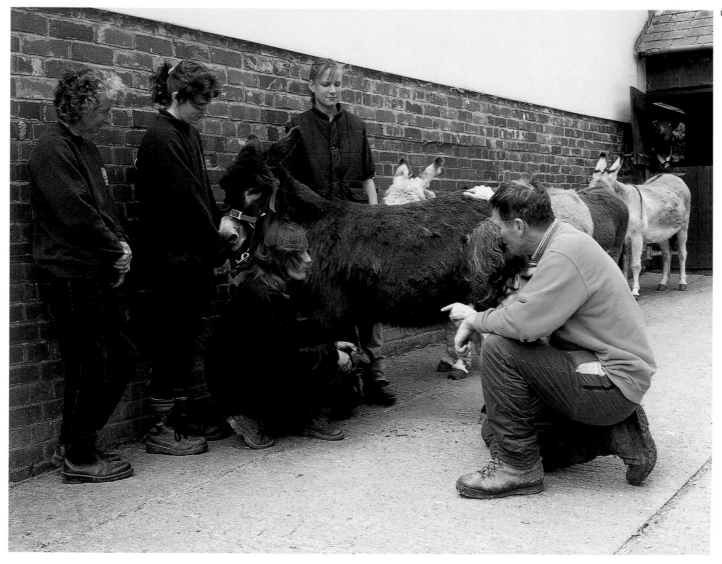

Young, fit and healthy donkeys can be fostered out to homes that have been strictly vetted by our welfare team. It's nice that they can belong to individual families and they have the benefit of being able to return to the Sanctuary in their old age, or if a problem arises in their adoptive home.

Before going to a new family the donkeys go to our Training Centre, which is not just for the donkeys, but for prospective owners! Before any donkey is placed in a new home the prospective owners have to attend a course at the Training Centre or one of our holding bases. It gives them a chance to see what will be involved and enables us to ensure that they have the basic knowledge required to give the donkey a really good home.

The Training Centre is also
used for the training of Welfare
Officers other than the 57 on
our staff. RSPCA Inspectors
are frequent students, and all
equine welfare charities are able
to take advantage of this free
training. We are great believers
in spreading donkey
knowledge in every way
possible, and our *Professional
Handbook of the Donkey* is used
throughout the world, a copy
being sent to every veterinary
university and to veterinary
surgeons upon request. It is the
only veterinary teaching book
on donkey care.

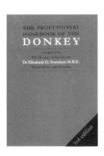

The Poitou donkeys are a special group. Our sister charity, the International Donkey Protection Trust, became involved in the preservation of this endangered species following requests from France in 1981. The group here causes immense interest from visitors - these gentle giants, with enormous ears and long, shaggy coats are the largest types of the donkey breed.

Many of our donkeys have come into our care as a result of ill-treatment, such as Lorcan (ABOVE, RIGHT), who had been chased by youths into a barbed wire fence, which had nearly ripped off his ears.

(RIGHT) But there's nothing wrong with Torrent's ears.

The arrival of another donkey in one of our specially adapted lorries can often give cause for concern. The driver generally communicates with us on his mobile phone when he has a particularly bad case, and a special 'reception committee' awaits the arrival. Often all our skills are needed as frightened donkeys arrive, obviously wondering what their new fate will be.

By mid-morning the main cleaning up is finished, and the routine rounds have been completed. An Administrator and the Farm Manager walk around the farm checking to see that the water troughs are spotlessly clean and full, and all the yards are tidy. A close eye is kept on all the donkeys, as they are often their own worst enemies! They are so stoic that they don't show symptoms of illness until the last moment, so it is vital that the staff in special charge of each group report any changes in a donkey's behaviour.

(LEFT) The field staff are busy - there are fields to plough, hay to make, hedges to trim and the beautiful walks around the Sanctuary to be kept in order. The large wintering barns have to be disinfected and cleaned ready for autumn.

(BELOW) 'Elephant Barn' is so named because of its size - I am standing right next to the tractor tyre!

Before Slade House Farm became
the Donkey Sanctuary, there were
few trees in the area, but our
consistent planting programme is
now helping to break the strong
winds that blow in from the sea,
as well as giving necessary shade
for the donkeys.

With so many donkeys, there has to be a problem with donkey dung (LEFT, BELOW) - literally thousands of tons are produced!! New legislation means we cannot let other farmers take the dung and spread it on their land, and we have to ensure that we don't cause any pollution. At the request of the Environment Agency, large willow beds are being made, where the 'dirty water' can be filtered naturally. These beds take up acres of land but, once established, they should solve our problems and provide a wonderful 'wet land' habitat for the benefit of all species of insects and animals.

There are many beautiful walks around the fields at the Sanctuary, along which our visitors can meander to see the donkeys. On these walks our supporters are able to dedicate a tree or a bench in memory of a loved one. Once a year, on 4th October, which is the day of the Feast of St Francis of Assisi, we hold a special Thanksgiving Service at Slade House Farm (which is also attended by some of our donkeys!), following which all the memorials are blessed by our local vicar, the Reverend Peter Leverton. (OUR MEMORIAL GARDEN IS SHOWN OPPOSITE, PICTURE TOP RIGHT)

The walks also enable the children who attend the E.S.T Sidmouth Centre to ride the donkeys round the track, with fresh air and lovely views, and a chance for the donkeys to see old friends in the fields as they pass!

(LEFT) Enjoying a beautiful Devon day at Woods Farm.

(RIGHT) A rather special set of eyebrows.

(LEFT) One of our handsome
Poitou donkeys.

Sometimes we stay very still,
only our tongues moving...

(LEFT) Sweet meadow hay is much appreciated.

(BELOW) Where's the champagne?

A good roll (BELOW) makes up
for the long winter months
when the donkeys stay in the
big wintering barns, warm and
dry.

(RIGHT) They all enjoy a fuss.

Donkeys come in many colours.

(RIGHT) And we have thousands of them!

(LEFT) Donkeys can be as smart as ponies when they are being driven.

(RIGHT) The Sanctuary staff always have time for an intimate chat.

58

To keep everything going requires firm organisation, and this is centred in Sidmouth. Expenses and administration costs are kept to a minimum, and efficiency is the order of the day. The staff are proud of the fact that 91.5 pence in every pound goes to the donkeys - as it should!

By tea-time another hard day's work has been done, the offices close down and the staff return home for a well earned rest. For the executives (RIGHT, BELOW), though, it could be a good time for a quiet meeting!

It's early evening. The evening staff are on duty until 10 p.m., when the night watchmen take over. Many of the donkeys are still quietly grazing, but some have already chosen their spot for the night and are laid out on the grass or in the large barns. Only the occasional flicker of an ear gives reassurance that the donkey is just sleeping - often their complete stillness can be alarming!

(RIGHT) We were worried, too!

An air of calm lies over the farms as night approaches. It seems strange after the bustle of the day. A donkey brays in the distance and another donkey nearly a mile across the valley answers back. Once again, peace reigns as darkness falls, and all is well in this donkey heaven.